NATIONAL FORUM ON EUROPE

Summary of the
Draft Constitutional Treaty
for the European Union

INCLUDING

Glossary of Terms

D0755880

SEPTEMBER 2003

The National Forum on Europe acknowledges
the financial support provided by the Communicating Europe Initiative
(under the aegis of the Department of Foreign Affairs)
towards the cost of producing this publication

NATIONAL FORUM ON EUROPE

FÓRAM NÁISIÚNTA UM AN EORAIP

Published by Stationery Office, Dublin, September 2003.
Designed by Ed Miliano. Printed by Brunswick Press.
Text printed on recycled paper.
To be purchased at the Government Publications Sale Office
Sun Alliance House, Molesworth Street, Dublin 2
€6.35

Table of Contents

Foreword

BY THE INDEPENDENT CHAIRMAN OF THE
NATIONAL FORUM ON EUROPE, SENATOR MAURICE HAYES

The National Forum on Europe decided last June that if and when the Convention on the Future of Europe agreed on a draft Constitutional Treaty for Europe, the Forum should produce a user-friendly summary, which would seek to set out the main elements in plain language that could be understood by the ordinary citizen. To help in this, it was agreed that the summary should have, with it, a glossary that would define and explain the more difficult 'Euro-jargon' phrases or words in the draft Treaty. This publication is the result of that decision.

It consists of three parts:
1. a short explanation of the background to the Convention on the Future of Europe and to the draft Treaty it produced;
2. a summary of the draft; and
3. a glossary of relevant 'Euro-jargon' terms.

The summary deals with the content of the draft, as it is, and, in the interests of keeping it short, does not, in general, compare the various elements with what was in earlier Treaties on the same subjects. The summary also seeks to be factual and thus avoids comments on the various elements. In seeking to compress a document containing 465 articles, 5 protocols and 3 declarations, it has not been possible to reflect every element and nuance. A considerable amount of selection was unavoidable: the Forum has sought to cover the most important elements, especially from an Irish perspective.

The role of the Forum is not to advocate any particular policy or course of action but rather to generate debate and to provide an arena for inclusive dialogue on matters relating to Ireland's role in the European Union. This publication is offered in that spirit. I hope that it will be accepted as objective information for the public and that it will help people to understand and to discuss the very important matters with which it deals.

I wish to express my appreciation for the work done by the Forum's secretariat in preparing this publication.

Background to the Draft Constitutional Treaty

". . . while remaining proud of their own national identities and history, the peoples of Europe are determined to transcend their ancient divisions and, united ever more closely, to forge a common destiny."

—from the preamble to the draft Constitutional Treaty

The foundational and fundamental rules and institutions of the European Union are set out in six principal treaties, negotiated between the Member States at various times throughout its history at what are known as Intergovernmental Conferences (IGCs).

A Convention was set up by the Cologne European Council in 1999 to discuss protection of Fundamental Rights in the EU. The Convention involved contributions from the governments and parliaments of the Member States as well as the European Parliament and the Commission. This was the first time in the history of the European Union that a process outside of an IGC was used to prepare such a document. The Convention adopted the Charter of Fundamental Rights on 2 October, 2000. The Presidents of the main EU institutions signed and proclaimed the Charter on 7 December, 2000 at the Nice summit.

That summit, resulting in the Treaty of Nice, not only paved the way for enlargement but also set the stage for a wide-ranging debate on the future development of the EU. One year later, the European Council, influenced by the success of the Charter of Fundamental Rights convention process and dissatisfaction with the traditional IGC process, adopted the Laeken Declaration, setting up the Convention on the Future of Europe. The Convention's mandate was to consider the key issues for the future development of an enlarged EU and to identify the various possible responses.

The Convention was made up of 105 members:
• a President (Valéry Giscard d'Estaing, former President of France), with two Vice-Presidents in Giuliano Amato and Jean-Luc Dehaene, respectively former Prime Ministers of Italy and Belgium;

• 15 representatives of the EU Heads of State and government;

• 13 representatives of the governments from the candidate countries;

• 30 representatives of the national parliaments of the EU countries (2 from each country);

• 26 representatives from the national parliaments of the candidate countries;

• 16 members of the European Parliament; and

• 2 representatives from the European Commission.

There were also 102 alternate members, as well as observers from the Economic and Social Committee (3), the Committee of the Regions (6), and the social partners (3), plus the European Ombudsman.

The Convention approach was widely seen as having made it possible for Treaty revision to take place, for the first time, in an open and transparent way. All plenary meetings of the Convention took place in public. All documents put before it, including all proposals for amendments to the treaties and in its later stages, for draft articles of a Constitutional Treaty were posted on the Convention Web site.

Another key element of the Convention process was an arena provided by the Convention for the participation of civil society, non-governmental and representative organisations and to stimulate reaction to the Convention's proceedings.

The Convention on the Future of Europe completed its work on 10 July, 2003 and presented its "Draft Treaty establishing a Constitution for Europe" to the Italian Presidency of the Council of Ministers on 18 July, 2003. The document represents a consolidation of all previous treaties but with some significant changes that are outlined in the summary that follows. As a constitutional treaty, *it would, if ratified by all Member States, exist alongside the constitutions of the Member States* and *would empower the EU to act only in specific areas.*

The draft Constitutional Treaty will go forward for discussion to an Intergovernmental Conference, which is to commence on 4 October, 2003.

Summary of the Draft Constitutional Treaty

INTRODUCTION

The draft Constitutional Treaty, if adopted by the IGC and ratified by the Member States, would replace treaties accumulated over fifty years with a single, new text, that is much more clear and readable. It is divided into four parts, introduced by a preamble.

• Part I is the core constitutional part. It defines the Union - its values, aims, powers, citizenship, decision-making rules, budgetary arrangements and institutions. It also contains provisions on joining the Union, suspension from it and withdrawal from it.

• Part 2 incorporates the Charter of Fundamental Rights, designed to protect citizens against EU laws that might infringe their basic rights. Up to now, the Charter has had no binding legal force: once the Constitutional Treaty took effect, the Charter would have such force.

• Part 3 consolidates the Articles from previous treaties dealing with all the Union's policies, into a single Constitutional Treaty. It also gives more detail than Part I in regard to the institutions, policy in the area of justice and home affairs, foreign policy, financial arrangements and decision-making.

• Part 4 sets out how Member States may go about ratifying and amending this new Constitutional Treaty.

A number of binding protocols are appended to the draft, including on
• principles as to when, and how far, the Union itself should take action within the domains where it shares powers with the Member States

• the future role of the national parliaments, including as guardian of those principles.

The Convention, short of time to consider all the protocols attached to previous Treaties, which would be repealed if the draft Constitutional Treaty were adopted, recommended that the IGC should decide what is to happen about these protocols. Such a review process, to include also declarations attached to the earlier treaties, is being considered. The earlier protocols and declarations that are of continuing direct relevance for Ireland are

– the protocol, attached to the Maastricht Treaty, relating to Article 40.3.3 of the Irish Constitution protecting the life of the unborn.

– the protocol, also attached to the Maastricht Treaty, on economic and social cohesion, which does not refer to Ireland by name but deals with issues relating to EU Structural Funds

– the protocol, attached to the Amsterdam Treaty, regarding the Schengen Agreement on free movement and related matters, and a related declaration by Ireland, designed to maintain the integrity of the long-established Common Travel Area with the UK.

Part I

VALUES AND AIMS
The draft Constitutional Treaty

Establishes the EU as
• a Union of the citizens and States of Europe

• open to all European States which respect its values and commit to promoting them together.

Outlines values on which the Union is based
• respect for human dignity, liberty, democracy, equality, the rule of law, respect for human rights, pluralism, tolerance, justice, solidarity and non-discrimination

Guarantees
• fundamental freedom of movement of goods, labour and capital and freedom to set up business anywhere in the Union

Declares that the aims of the Union are (among other things) to …
• promote peace, its values and the well-being of its peoples

• offer its citizens an area of freedom, security and justice without internal frontiers

• achieve economic growth, aiming at full employment and social progress, with a high level of protection of the environment

• respect its rich cultural and linguistic diversity

• show solidarity between Member States and regions and advance reduction of economic and social inequalities between them

• combat social exclusion and discrimination

• promote social justice and protection, equality between men and women, solidarity between generations and children's rights.

… and in its relations with the wider world, that its aims include to
• contribute to peace, security, free and fair trade and sustainable development

• eradicate poverty and protect human rights and, in particular, children's rights

• strictly observe international law, including respect for the principles of the United Nations Charter.

The draft Constitutional Treaty sets out how to achieve these aims
• by giving the Union powers to act for the whole Union, conferred on it in defined areas by the Member States
 – in return, it pledges that the Union would respect the national identity of its Member States, as reflected in their constitutional and regional structures. It would not interfere with essential functions of the State, including law and order and territorial integrity

• by making the Union a single legal entity instead of the confusing legal amalgam it is now. This, and other changes, would make it easier to negotiate and ratify international agreements and thus to assert its values and interests internationally.

Belonging To The Union

Joining the Union

For a State to join the Union, a unanimous Council decision is required, together with the approval of the European Parliament and ratification of the agreement about joining by all pre-existing Member States.

Suspension From the Union

On a proposal by at least one-third of Member States, or the Commission or the European Parliament, the Council of Ministers, by a four-fifths majority of its membership, could decide, after obtaining the consent of the European Parliament, that there was a clear risk of a breach by a Member State of the Union's values. In a further step up, the *European Council*, acting on a proposal by at least one-third of Member States or by the Commission, *could unanimously decide*, after obtaining the consent of the European Parliament, that *there was a serious and persistent breach* of *the Union's values* by a Member State. Once any such decision was taken, *a further decision by the Council* of Ministers, by Qualified Majority Voting (QMV), *could suspend* certain *rights of the Member State in question, including Council voting rights.*

Voluntary Withdrawal From the Union

The draft Constitutional Treaty introduces the possibility of voluntary withdrawal from the EU, something no previous treaty has foreseen. Should a Member State decide to withdraw, it would notify the Council of its decision. The Union would then negotiate an agreement with the Member State concerned, detailing the arrangements for the withdrawal and outlining the relationship between the Member State and the Union after withdrawal. That agreement would be concluded on behalf of the Union by the Council, acting by QMV, after obtaining the assent of the European Parliament. The withdrawing State would not participate in the Council's discussions or decisions concerning it.

CITIZENSHIP AND RIGHTS

The draft Constitutional Treaty defines *citizens of the Union* as
• every national of a Member State

• having the right, among others, to move freely within the Union, to vote and stand for election to the European Parliament and local elections in any Member State

• entitled to get consular protection in other countries from the embassies of EU partner countries.

Another section of Part I, on 'The Democratic Life of the Union' sets down the following guiding principles
• the principle of democratic equality—all citizens equal and to receive equal attention from EU institutions

• the principle of representative democracy—members of EU institutions directly elected by the people or accountable to elected national parliaments or the European Parliament

• the principle of participatory democracy—Union institutions to maintain an open, transparent and regular dialogue with civil society and its associations

• the principle of popular initiative—one million citizens across a significant number of Member States could ask the Commission to propose action in an area covered by the draft Constitutional Treaty.

• the Union would continue to recognize and promote the role of the social partners at Union level and would facilitate dialogue between them

• the Union would respect (the status of) churches and religious associations or communities

• it would equally respect the status of philosophical and non-confessional organisations

To be more transparent to citizens
• the Union institutions would do their work as openly as possible

• the Council of Ministers would, like the Parliament, meet in public when making laws

• citizens would have a right of access of EU documents, while having their own personal data protected from disclosure.

Fundamental rights of citizens would be guaranteed in respect of the Union's actions
• the Union would ask to join the European Convention on Human Rights

• basic rights stemming from the constitutional traditions the Member States share would also be general principles of the Union's law

• the Charter of Fundamental Rights would be binding (see Part II, page 36).

POWERS—WHO COULD DO WHAT?

The draft states explicitly that the Union draws its powers from Member States, rather than the other way around. It says clearly that powers not given to the Union would remain with the Member States. *It defines where the EU could and could not act*—how far decisions would have to be agreed at EU level or could be taken by a Member State on its own: in general, the fields covered by the EU would only be slightly extended.

Exclusive Powers

When action at Union level is accepted as more effective than separate action by each of the Member States, only the Union would act on behalf of all, in areas like
• Competition rules within the single market

- Monetary policy for eurozone members
- Common trade policy and customs union
- Conservation of fish

Shared Powers

The Union would share decision-making with Member States in areas like

- Agriculture and Fisheries
- Asylum and Immigration
- Judicial and Policing co-operation
- The internal market
- Transport
- The environment
- Regional, and some aspects of social, policies
- Consumer protection
- Research, technology and space
- Aid to developing countries
- Other areas covered in the summary of Part IV (page 44)

Supporting Role

The Union would have only a supporting role in areas like

- Education and Training
- Health
- Culture
- Sport and Youth
- Industry

In these areas, the main role would remain with Member States. A limit is put to the type of legally binding acts the Union could take in these areas: such acts could not seek to harmonise the laws or regulations of the Member States.

Co-ordinator

In the interests of overall efficiency, the Union could coordinate the policies of Member States, in

• Policy on jobs, the economy and the social field
but here, too, imposed harmonisation of national laws would be excluded.

Foreign Policy
The Union would also have the power, as it has had since the Maastricht Treaty of 1992, to pursue a common foreign and security policy.

Flexibility Clause
If the Union needed to act to pursue a policy objective allowed for in the Constitutional Treaty but the Treaty had not given it the power to do so, it could do so only with the unanimous approval of the Member States. This is called a flexibility clause. National Parliaments would be able to monitor and influence the use of this clause.

THE INSTITUTIONS WHICH RUN THE UNION
The draft Constitutional Treaty reiterates that the Union will be run by five main institutions[1] working in co-operation.
• The European Parliament
• The European Council
• The Council of Ministers
• The European Commission
• The Court of Justice

The European Parliament
The European Parliament represents the people of all the Member States. Under the draft Constitutional Treaty, it would
• *elect its own President* and officers

• continue to be *directly elected by the citizens* of the Union every five years

• have a *maximum of 736 members*, with national representation broadly

---

1. In what follows about the institutions, account has been taken of provisions included in Part III of the draft Constitutional Treaty and in protocols appended to it.

proportional to population size, but with more favourable treatment, the smaller the Member State: Ireland would have 13 MEPs. If and when Bulgaria and Romania join, this would go down to 12 after 2009.

• have *44 more areas* in which it acts as *co-legislator* with the Council of Ministers

• continue to *approve the EU budget*, alongside the Council

• continue to have some *political control over the European Commission* (for example, approving or dismissing the President and other members of that body)

• continue to *appoint an European Ombudsman.*

Under the draft Constitutional Treaty, the Council of Ministers will, before the June 2009 elections, decide unanimously on the national allocations of seats for the 2009-2014 term of the Parliament.

The European Council
The European Council is made up of the most senior politicians representing the Member States—*Prime Ministers and Presidents.* It meets at least four times a year. It gives the Union its political direction and sets its priorities.

Under the draft Constitutional Treaty, the European Council would be composed of
• The President of the European Council
• The Union Minister for Foreign Affairs
• Heads of State or Government of the Member States
• The President of the European Commission.

The President of the European Council
• *is a newly-created position which would put a person rather than a country in*

the chair of the Council (until now, the European Council has been chaired by the Member State holding the rotating six-month Presidency of the Union)
• would be *elected by the European Council* for a period of *two and half years*, renewable once

• would *drive its work and represent the Union abroad,* at the highest level, more or less as the rotating Presidents sought to do up to now

• could *not hold any national position:* a serving Prime Minister could not have the position.

The Union Minister for Foreign Affairs
• is *another new position, to operate from 2009,* on the basis of what is in the draft Treaty

• would represent the EU in the political, diplomatic, trade and aid arenas, replacing the two people who cover these areas now

• would "put a face on" EU foreign policy—make it more identifiable, cohesive and effective

• would "wear two hats", one as a Vice-President of the Commission and thus part of its team, for the trade and aid aspects, and the second, reporting to the Foreign Affairs Council on the political and diplomatic aspects.

The European Council would make decisions by consensus and would not pass laws.

The Council of Ministers
The Council of Ministers is where government ministers of the Member States meet to pass laws to advance the common Union interest, while promoting or defending their national interests. Under the draft Constitutional Treaty, the Council of Ministers

• would continue to be made up of one minister for each relevant portfolio from every Member State. The draft proposes the creation of a "General Affairs and Legislative Council" and a "Foreign Affairs Council" and also that the European Council decide on what will in future be the other Council formations e.g. Finance Ministers, Agriculture Ministers, etc.

• would have new arrangements for rotating its Presidency. Instead of the relevant minister from the country holding the rotating EU Presidency occupying the chair for the six months of its Presidency, it would now be held for a period of at least a year. There would still be equal rotation between the Member States but the chairs of different Council formations might no longer be all held by ministers from the same country at the same time. The chair of the Council for Foreign Affairs would not rotate. Instead, it would be chaired by the "permanent" new Union Foreign Affairs Minister

• would have a simplified voting system (see section on More Legitimate and Effective Decision-Making, page 26).

The European Commission
• represents the interests of the Union as a whole and is often perceived as the guardian of the interests of the smaller countries

• proposes the laws on which the European Parliament and Council of Ministers have to take a decision

• administers the budget and manages the Community programmes

• seeks to ensure that EU treaties, laws, rules and decisions are complied with

• negotiates for the Union in the international trade and aid areas.

All this would continue.

Because any new Constitutional Treaty would not be ratified and in operation by November, 2004, when the next Commission is to take office and because, by then, the Union will have less than 27 members, the appointment of the Commission President and the other Commissioners will take place under the arrangements set out in the Treaty of Nice for a Union of less than 27 members

• each of the then 25 Member States will have one Commissioner

• the Council of Ministers, meeting at the level of Heads of State or Government, will nominate the President-elect, deciding by QMV

• the Council of Ministers, again by QMV, will agree the list of Commissioners nominated by the Member States

• the full nominated Commission will be submitted to the European Parliament for a vote of approval.

From November 2009 the system would change. With 25-plus member countries, the Commission would be made up as follows

• the President of the Commission—nominated on the basis of QMV by the European Council and elected by the European Parliament

• the new Union Minister for Foreign Affairs who would be a Vice-President of the Commission

• thirteen "European Commissioners", selected on *an equal rotation basis* between the Member States, by the President-elect picking from lists of three candidates presented by each Member State (including at least one man and one woman)

• the remaining Member States, in any term, would have non-voting "Commissioners".

Once this new system took effect, the European Council would have to take account of the results of the European Parliament elections (e.g. as to the relative success of different political groupings) when proposing a candidate for election as Commission President. For the first time, the European Parliament would be able, legally, to elect or reject the nominee for President. In the case of rejection, the procedure would be re-run, with a fresh candidate. The Parliament would continue to have the legal right to approve or reject the proposed membership of the Commission, as a body.

The Commission would continue, at all stages, to take decisions by a simple majority of its members. The allocation of portfolios would be a matter for the Commission President, who could also reshuffle.

The Court of Justice
The Court of Justice, comprising mainly the European Court of Justice, which would be supported by a High Court, would continue to be the institution responsible for interpreting and enforcing Union law.

Under the draft Constitutional Treaty
• the name of the High Court would be simpler

• there would still be judges appointed to the two main constituent courts from all the Member States, including the enlargement countries—one per Member State

• it should be easier for the public to take actions against EU laws even if they do not affect them individually, as was a condition up to now

• the Court could more easily impose penalties and fines and thus penalize more quickly Member States in breach of EU law or obligations.

Other EU Bodies

The draft Constitutional Treaty also consolidates what was in previous treaties about the European Central Bank, the European System of Central Banks, the Court of Auditors, the two advisory bodies—the Economic and Social Committee and the Committee of the Regions—and the European Investment Bank.

SIMPLIFYING THE RULES

The proposed changes to the institutions are aimed at making them more democratic, transparent and effective. The *other big objective* of the debate on the future of Europe *is to simplify* the way the EU does business.

Under the draft Constitutional Treaty, the number of legal instruments would be reduced from 15 to 6 and their names would be changed to more familiar terms. Thus, laws passed at European level would be called European Laws and European Framework Laws

• *European Laws* (previously "Regulations") would be binding and apply directly in all Member States

• *European Framework Laws* (previously "Directives") would also be binding but Member States would be free to choose the ways to implement them.

The present legal instruments, *Recommendations* and *Opinions* would remain but would continue to have no binding force. Another instrument to continue would be Decisions—renamed *European Decisions.* These would not be laws but would be binding.

The sixth instrument would be a *European regulation*. This would be analogous to statutory instruments or Ministerial orders in Ireland and be concerned with the detailed implementation of European Laws or Framework Laws.

The general rule would be that European legislation would be decided by the Council of Ministers and the European Parliament interacting on an equal footing, on the basis of proposals made by the Commission. In the great majority of areas, only the Commission could put forward proposals. These arrangements are termed, in the draft, the *ordinary legislative procedure.*

There are a small number of exceptions. Foreign policy is one. Here, EU laws would be excluded and separate, specific decision-making procedures would apply. In the domestic area, a quarter of Member States would also be able to make proposals on
  – judicial co-operation in criminal matters
  – police co-operation

In all the fields in which Member States confer powers on the Union, *the Constitutional Treaty and EU law adopted under it would have primacy over national law, as with EU treaties to date.*

MORE LEGITIMATE AND EFFECTIVE DECISION-MAKING
As part of the drive for simplification but also in order to make the operation of the Union more effective and more legitimate, the draft Constitutional Treaty and protocols[1] attached to it significantly strengthen principles first set down in earlier treaties and streamline how decisions would be made.

Principles That EU Law-Making Must Respect
The use of EU powers would be governed by two principles
• **subsidiarity** and **proportionality**

Under the *principle of subsidiarity*[2], the Union would act at all, only if it could be shown that the objectives in view could not be sufficiently achieved by the

---

1. In what follows about decision-making, account has been taken of provisions included in Part III of the draft Constitutional Treaty and in the protocols attached to it.
2. Clearly, this principle relates to cases where either the Union or the Member States could act— and not to areas where the Union has exclusive powers.

Member States, at central, regional or local level but could be better achieved at EU level.

Under the *principle of proportionality*, the type and substance of EU action should not go any further than what is necessary to achieve the aims of the Constitutional Treaty e.g. a law should not be proposed where a recommendation would do: if a law is needed, it should only cover what is strictly necessary. A legally binding protocol lays down how these principles are to be applied in detail.

Enhanced Role for National Parliaments

The same protocol and a second one also set down a set of rules to strengthen the role of national parliaments in the whole EU law-making process. Many of these rules relate to procedures for circulation of documents and minimum periods before decisions could be taken. However, for the first time, national parliaments will be able to issue opinions (or put in more colloquial terms, 'show a yellow card') if they think proposals for EU laws or other actions go against subsidiarity. If one-third[1], at least, of the parliaments took this view, the Commission would have to re-consider its proposal and could maintain, amend or withdraw it.

As a last resort, national parliaments or Member State governments or, in cases relevant to its functions, the Committee of the Regions, would have the power to refer their concerns about any breach of subsidiarity to the European Court of Justice, for a binding ruling.

Changes In How Decisions Would Be Made

Under the draft Constitutional Treaty, the broad lines of the system for taking decisions would not change much. The roles of the institutions would be as set out above and the balance of power between them would remain broadly the same.

---

1. One quarter, in the case of proposals in the fields of judicial co-operation in criminal matters or police co-operation.

However,

• the European Parliament would gain an equal footing with the Council of Ministers in an additional 44 areas

• the voting system in the Council of Ministers would change from unanimity to QMV in 23 more areas. However, there is also an article which would allow the European Council, by a unanimous decision, to agree that henceforth QMV would apply in an area still left, under the draft Constitutional Treaty, to unanimity, without having to ratify a further treaty

• until 2009, the definition of QMV in the Treaty of Nice would continue to apply. From 1 November 2009, a new, simpler, definition of QMV would come into operation. From then on, a simple majority of Member States, representing three-fifths, or more, of the EU's population, would count as a qualified majority

• the need for a unanimous vote would remain in almost 60 cases, even after 2009.

ENHANCED CO-OPERATION

The draft Constitutional Treaty incorporates what was in the Treaty of Nice about 'enhanced co-operation'. This relates to a particular set of arrangements *where some Member States, but not all, want to co-operate more closely in a particular area.*

Enhanced co-operation

• needs to involve at least one-third of Member States wanting to go ahead

• would have to be open, then and later, to all Member States

• would have to get the backing of the Commission, be approved by the Council of Ministers and be accepted by the European Parliament, where it related to internal EU matters

• would have to get the backing of the Union Foreign Minister and of the Commission, and be approved by the Council of Ministers, where it related to common foreign and security policy

• could only be a last resort, where it is clear that the objectives in view could not be achieved by the Union as a whole within a reasonable timeframe

• would have to
 – avoid undermining the single market or regional policy in the Union
 – not be a barrier to, or lead to discrimination in trade between, Member States
 – not distort competition.

Under the draft Constitutional Treaty, the previous ban on enhanced co-operation being used in the security and defence area no longer applies.

COMMON FOREIGN AND SECURITY POLICY[1] (CFSP)

The draft Constitutional Treaty proposes significant changes in the way the EU would conduct its foreign and security policy (political, diplomatic, trade and aid), in future.

Under the proposals
• All the foreign policy provisions in all the Treaties have been grouped together, making them more readable and accessible

• A new post of *Union Minister for Foreign Affairs* is proposed
 – to represent the Union giving it a stronger, more effective voice on the international stage (he/she will be in charge of a foreign service with delegations in around 125 countries)
 – to put into effect the common foreign and security policy, "using national and union resources".

---

1. In what follows about the Common Foreign and Security Policy account has been taken of provisions included in Part III of the draft Constitutional Treaty.

– to coordinate all the Union's external action, including Union positions at international organisations and conferences, which he/she would express – so that when the United Nations Security Council is debating an issue on which the EU has a position, those Member States which sit on the Council must request that the Minister be asked to present the EU's position.

In other respects, the proposals largely consolidate what is in the earlier Treaties

• the European Council would identify the EU's strategic interests and decide the objectives of its Common Foreign and Security Policy

• the Council of Ministers would frame the policy within that context

• decisions would, in general, continue to be by unanimity. However, there would be two exceptions. Firstly, the draft specifically provides for the possibility of QMV where a particular decision relates to a policy previously decided at summit level or, alternatively, to details of implementation. But, even in these cases, a Member State could, for vital and stated reasons of national policy, veto any resort to decision by QMV. Secondly, there is a general clause, under which the European Council could decide unanimously to transfer decisions in any Common Foreign and Security Policy domain, *other than military and defence aspects* from the unanimity to the QMV category

• the European Parliament would continue to be consulted and informed on important Common Foreign and Security Policy aspects

• Member States would be bound to support the Union's Common Foreign and Security Policy and not to impede its implementation. They would also have to consult each other or major foreign and security policy issues, especially before undertaking any actions or commitments that could affect the common interests of the Union.

COMMON SECURITY AND DEFENCE POLICY[1] (CSDP)

The draft Constitutional Treaty says that the common security and defence policy
• would be an integral part of EU foreign policy

• would enable the Union to draw on civil and military resources provided by the Member States to take part in missions *outside its borders.* These would be
- joint disarmament operations
- humanitarian and rescue tasks
- military advice and assistance tasks
- conflict prevention
- peace-keeping
- tasks of combat forces in crisis management (including peacemaking and post-conflict stabilisation).
- to strengthen international security, in line with the principles of the United Nations Charter.

Such missions would only be authorised by a unanimous vote of the Council of Ministers on a proposal from the Union Foreign Affairs Minister or a Member State.

The draft Constitutional Treaty would, however, allow for those Member States with bigger military capabilities to commit to taking part together in the most demanding missions within the *external* tasks listed above.

This will be called
• *"Structured Co-operation".*

Only the ministers of those Member States taking part in this arrangement would be allowed to debate and vote in the Council of Ministers on any action proposed under this pact.

---

1. In what follows about the Common Security and Defence Policy account has been taken of provisions included in Part III of the draft Constitutional Treaty.

In regard to *defence of the EU and its Member States*, the draft Constitutional Treaty also explicitly states that the security and defence policy will include the progressive framing of a common defence policy and that this *"will lead to a common defence"* when the European Council unanimously so decides. Any such decision would have to be ratified constitutionally—which, should Ireland wish to participate in such a common defence, would require a 'yes' in a referendum.

Any policy in this area
• would respect the neutrality of Member States like Ireland

• would respect the obligations of other Members States which are part of NATO and fit in with the security and defence policy established in that framework.

Pending any European Council decision to move to a common defence against external aggression, the draft Constitutional Treaty provides for
• *"Closer co-operation"* between willing Member States on mutual defence—this would oblige those States to go to the aid of a fellow EU country which was a participant in such co-operation and came under armed aggression.

Under the draft Constitutional Treaty, an *Armaments, Research and Military Capabilities Agency* would be set up that
• would be open to all Member States *"wishing to be part of it"*

• would seek to improve, streamline and evaluate the military capabilities of the participating Member States.

Under the proposals, the European Parliament would be regularly consulted on and informed of the main developments in the common security and defence policy.

The draft Constitutional Treaty introduces a new area of solidarity that would be expected of all EU members. The *Solidarity Clause* says that
• the Union and its Member States would act jointly in a spirit of solidarity if a Member State were the victim of terrorist attack or natural or man-made disaster

• the Union would mobilise all its resources, civil and military, to:
   – *prevent the terrorist threat in the territory of the Member States*
   – *protect* democratic *institutions* and the *civilian population* from any terrorist attack
   – *assist a Member State in its territory* at the request of its political authorities *if a terrorist attack happened*
   – *assist a Member State in its territory* at the request of its political authorities *in the event of a disaster.*

The precise arrangements for putting this clause into effect would be settled unanimously by the Council of Ministers, on the basis of a joint proposal by the Commission and the Union Foreign Minister.

PROTECTING THE UNION'S CITIZENS AT HOME

The European Union defines itself as an area of freedom, security and justice. So how do you allow people to move freely across borders while protecting the Union from terrorism and serious crime?

The draft Constitutional Treaty sets out to do this by including provisions that would
• give the Union more powers in the justice and home affairs area

• enhance the Union's effectiveness in fields where it has already been active—external border control, visas, asylum and immigration

• extend the Union's field of action to the fight against serious cross-border crime, police co-operation, mutual recognition of decisions by courts and judges and make possible the future creation of a Union public prosecutor, with functions in defined areas.

It is proposed that the Union would
• ensure the absence of border controls inside the Union

• frame a common policy, including passing European laws or framework laws, on asylum, immigration and control at the Union's outside borders, based on solidarity, financially and otherwise, between Member States and also fairness to the people of countries outside the Union

• promote and take measures to prevent and fight crime, racism and hatred of foreigners and for co-operation between police forces, prosecutors, courts and judges; and also by mutual recognition of judgments in criminal matters and, if needed, bringing Member States' criminal laws closer together

• promote access to justice, especially by mutual recognition of decisions in Member States in civil law matters, including through, for the first time, the passing of European laws or framework laws.

Under the previous treaties, the Union could already act in the areas of *police co-operation and judicial co-operation on criminal matters*, but under inter-governmental co-operation methods rather than the normal 'Community method'. Under the proposals in the draft Constitutional Treaty, the handling of these areas would be more in line with normal EU procedures, where the Commission makes proposals, the European Parliament and Council of Ministers co-legislate on an equal footing and the rules adopted are subject to the scrutiny of the Court of Justice. One special feature: a quarter of Member States could propose a measure, in the same way as the Commission.

As regards *judicial co-operation in criminal matters*, the Council of Ministers could pass European framework laws setting down minimum rules for the *definition of offences* and for *penalties* in regard to listed serious and cross-border offences—organized crime, terrorism, trafficking in human beings, sexual exploitation of women and children, drugs and arms trafficking, money laundering, counterfeiting, computer crime and corruption.

Under the proposals, the Union could also pass framework laws on *criminal procedure*, setting down minimum rules with regard to the rights of individuals in such procedure and the rights of victims—but adoption of such rules would not prevent Member States from maintaining or introducing a higher standard of protection for the rights of individuals.

The mechanisms for judicial co-operation in this field, such as *Eurojust*, would be strengthened but also, for the first time, made subject to evaluation by the European Parliament and national parliaments. At some time in the future, the Council of Ministers could decide, by unanimous vote, to set up a European Public Prosecutor's Office to track down and prosecute the perpetrators of, and accomplices in, serious cross-border crimes.

The draft Constitutional Treaty consolidates pre-existing provisions governing *Europol* which is a structure for developing police co-operation between Member States in preventing and combating all serious forms of organized international crime; but it also provides, for the first time, that Europol, too, would be subject to evaluation by the European Parliament and national parliaments.

THE UNION'S FINANCES AND BUDGET

In general, the draft Constitutional Treaty consolidates what was in previous treaties about the Union's finances and budget but also includes provisions under which the EU budget would henceforth be adopted by the European Parliament and the Council of Ministers by a much simpler procedure than applies now.

Part II

The Charter of Fundamental Rights

The text of the Charter of Fundamental Rights had been agreed by a previous widely representative Convention. However, up until now, the Charter has not been part of the Union's Treaties and had no binding legal force.

Under the draft Constitutional Treaty, of which it would now be Part II, it *would* have binding legal force

• the institutions, bodies and agencies of the Union would have to respect the rights written into the Charter.

• the same obligations would be incumbent upon the *Member States only when they were implementing the Union's legislation*

• the Court of Justice would ensure that the Charter is adhered to.

However, inclusion of the Charter would not give the Union extra powers, or affect the balance between its area of operation and that of the Member States. Relevant provisions in the draft Constitutional Treaty include

• Part II explicitly says that it "does not extend the field of application of Union law beyond the powers of the Union or establish any new power or task for the Union"

• it states that full account is to be taken of national laws and practices

• it says that nothing in the Charter is to be interpreted as restricting or adversely affecting human rights, as recognized by, inter alia, the Member States' constitutions.

The content of the Charter is broader than that of the 1950 European Convention for the Protection of Human Rights and Fundamental Freedoms (EHCR). It draws on the previous European Social Charters worked out by both the EU and the Council of Europe. While the ECHR is limited to civil and political rights, the Charter of Fundamental Rights covers other areas such as
• the right to proper administration
• social rights
• the protection of personal data
• bioethics.

The rights under the Charter, as now incorporated, apply to every person in the EU except where it is stated that they are 'citizens rights' and thus apply only to those who are EU citizens.

The draft Constitutional Treaty fully incorporates the Charter, setting out under the following headings the 54 Articles, which are clear and succinct (see Part II of the draft Constitutional Treaty).

Dignity
• Human dignity
• Right to life
• Right to the integrity of the person
• Prohibition of torture and inhuman or degrading treatment or punishment
• Prohibition of slavery and forced labour

Freedoms
- Right to liberty and security
- Respect for private and family life
- Protection of personal data
- Right to marry and right to found a family
- Freedom of thought, conscience and religion
- Freedom of expression and information
- Freedom of assembly and of association
- Freedom of the arts and sciences
- Right to education
- Freedom to choose an occupation and right to engage in work
- Freedom to conduct a business
- Right to property
- Right to asylum
- Protection in the event of removal, expulsion or extradition

Equality
- Equality before the law
- Non-discrimination
- Cultural, religious and linguistic diversity
- Equality between men and women
- The rights of the child
- The rights of the elderly
- Integration of persons with disabilities

Solidarity
- Workers' right to information and consultation (within the undertaking)
- Right of collective bargaining and action
- Right of access to placement services
- Protection in the event of unjustified dismissal
- Fair and just working conditions
- Prohibition of child labour and protection of young people at work
- Family and professional life

• Social security and social assistance
• Health care
• Access to services of general economic interest
• Environmental protection
• Consumer protection

Citizens' Rights
• Right to vote and to stand as a candidate at elections to the European Parliament in any Member State
• Right to vote and to stand as a candidate at municipal elections in any Member State
• Right to good EU administration
• Right of access to documents
• European Ombudsman
• Right to petition the European Parliament
• Freedom of movement and of residence
• Diplomatic and consular protection

Justice
• Right to an effective remedy and to a fair trial
• Presumption of innocence and right of defence
• Principles of legality and proportionality of criminal offences and penalties
• Right not to be tried or punished twice in criminal proceedings for the same criminal offence

Part III

This part contains 342 articles, about three-quarters of the total number and deals with the policies and functioning of the Union. It very largely reproduces the Articles from previous Treaties which set out the provisions governing the Union's policies in all the different areas, such as free movement of goods, services, persons and capital, employment, social policy, regional policy, agriculture and fisheries, environment, transport, etc. As a general rule, there were no significant changes to these policies and only very limited extensions of the Union's field of activity. Thus, for most articles in this part, the only changes from previous treaties are to fit them into a more logical layout and, in that connection, to renumber them. Little point would be served by seeking to summarise this voluminous material.

Other elements in Part III involved spelling out, in a more detailed way, aspects of matters dealt with in Part I—the functioning of the institutions, the operation of a common foreign and security policy, common security and defence policy and the 'area of freedom, security and justice'. The most relevant provisions under these headings have been summarised above, in conjunction with the summarisation of the related elements of Part I—this seemed the most convenient procedure for readers. In what follows, the main remaining elements in Part III are summarised.

Clauses of General Application
• A short series of articles seeks to ensure that wider Union objectives —gender equality, opposition to discrimination on multiple grounds, protection of the environment, consumer protection, reduction of regional disparities, wide-

spread access to services of general economic interest—are taken fully into account when defining and implementing each specific policy of the Union

• Provision is made for the adoption of European laws or framework laws, if and as necessary, to combat discrimination on any of a range of grounds; to facilitate the exercise of the right to move and reside freely within the Union; and to fix the detailed arrangements for the exercise of the rights of European citizens to vote, where they live, in European Parliament and local elections.

• An article clarifies in which languages citizens have a right to address, and get a reply from, the Union institutions and advisory bodies—these include the Irish language.

Changes in Decision-Making Procedures
• In 23 Articles, where previously Council of Ministers decision were by unanimity, they would, for the future, be on the basis of QMV. In most such cases, the European Parliament would now be a co-legislator, on an equal footing with the Council of Ministers, where, up to now, the Parliament was simply consulted.

• While unanimity voting was retained for decisions on all taxation matters, the following innovations were agreed—measures on indirect taxes, such as VAT and excise duties, or on company taxation, could be adopted in future by QMV in the Council of Ministers, *if Ministers first agree, by unanimity*, that any such measures relate only to administrative co-operation or to combating tax fraud and tax evasion.

• The European Parliament would get an enhanced role in relation to negotiations on trade with other countries or in the World Trade Organisation. Up to now, it had no legal basis for a role in decision-making or even monitoring such negotiations. Under the new proposals, the Commission would have to report to the Parliament as well as to a special committee of the Council of Ministers on the progress of negotiations, while Council and Parliament would jointly pass the laws required to implement the Union's common policy on trade.

• The previous position on services of general economic interest has been strengthened, so that the Union would be able to pass European laws defining principles and conditions for the operation of such services, which would enable them to fulfil their missions.

Introduction of new legal bases
• The draft Constitutional Treaty proposes new legal bases which would allow the Union to take action in
  – the area of public health, in response to wider concerns affecting the safety of the general public
  – energy
  – dealing with natural or man-made disasters
  – sport
  – space policy

Changes in Economic Governance Field
• The draft Constitutional Treaty proposes to strengthen the powers of the European Commission regarding implementation of the excessive deficit procedure of the Stability and Growth Pact. In the future, the Council of Ministers would only be able to diverge from a Commission *proposal* concerning the existence of an excessive deficit, by unanimous vote, as opposed to the present situation where the Commission *makes a recommendation* which Finance Ministers do not have to accept

• The proposals also include a new set of articles specific to Member States which are part of the Euro area. A related protocol is annexed to the draft Constitutional Treaty, under which
  – provision is proposed for specific economic policy guidelines for those Member States
  – provision is made for the Eurozone ministers to settle common positions

on matters arising in international financial institutions and conferences that are relevant to the euro and its management
– provision is made whereby the informal grouping of Eurozone Finance Ministers would have an elected President for a 2 1/2 year period, replacing the rotation system that operated up to now.

Part IV

What Is In This Part

This part deals with legal, mainly technical, aspects relating to

• the repeal of the earlier treaties that the draft Constitutional Treaty would, if ratified, take over from

• legal continuity as between matters settled under the various treaties, as they were up to now and the new Constitutional Treaty that, if ratified, would replace them

• what countries and territories the draft Constitutional Treaty would and would not apply to

• the status of protocols to the draft Treaty—that they would have full legal force

• the procedure for revising, in future, the draft Constitutional Treaty

• the requirements for the adoption, ratification and entry into force of the draft Treaty

• its duration—for an unlimited period

• the languages in which it would, if ratified, be equally authentic – including the Irish language

• the symbols of the Union – its flag, anthem, motto, currency and special day.

Procedure for Future Amendments

The government of any Member State, the European Parliament or the Commission could propose amendments to the draft Constitutional Treaty. The decision as to whether to examine any proposed amendments would be taken by the European Council, by a simple majority, after consulting the European Parliament.

If the European Council said "no", that would be the end for the proposed amendment. If its answer was "yes", its President would have to convene a Convention, with membership as inclusive as in the Convention on the Future of Europe. However, if they decided, again by a simple majority, that the proposed amendments were not important enough to warrant calling a Convention, it would be for an IGC to do this work. Where a Convention *was* held, it would adopt a consensus recommendation on the proposed amendments. This would then be considered by an *IGC*, which *would*, as now, *have to reach a unanimous decision*. Also, as now, before any amendments could enter into force, *they would have to be ratified by all Member States*.

**Adoption, Ratification and Entry Into Force
of the Draft Constitutional Treaty**

There is *no change, from* what applied with *previous Treaties, as regards the entry into force of the draft Constitutional Treaty*. This could only happen if it were ratified by all of the Member States, which will then be at least 25.

If, however, by two years after the draft Treaty was signed, at least four-fifths of Member States had ratified it and one or more others had met difficulties in doing so, the matter would have to be referred to the European Council, to consider what to do.

Glossary of Terms

EXPLANATORY NOTE

The terms explained in this glossary are, in general, ones that occur in the draft Constitutional Treaty, where the meaning may not be clear to the ordinary person who is not an expert on European affairs and where it is not explained fully in the text of the summary. A small number of other words or phrases which often arise in discussions about the matters dealt with in the draft Constitutional Treaty are also included.

Accountability
The capacity or duty to account in an open, transparent manner for actions taken, or not taken, whether by an individual or an institution.

Appropriations
In the EU context, this is a term relating to the budget and refers to amounts of money to be committed to be spent at some time in the next short period of years (commitment appropriations) or actually to be spent in the current or forthcoming financial year (expenditure appropriations).

(To) Approximate (National Laws)
This means to bring about a situation where the law applying in certain areas of life in the different Member States is more closely similar but not necessarily exactly the same.

Charter of Fundamental Rights

This Charter, adopted by an earlier Convention in October 2000, sets out in a single text, for the first time in the European Union's history, civil, political, economic and social rights and freedoms of European citizens and all persons resident in the EU. Before its adoption, these rights were laid down in a variety of national, European and international sources. The Charter has been incorporated into the draft Constitutional Treaty as Part II. It would apply to the Union's Institutions and to the Member States' governments only when they were implementing Union law.

Common Foreign and Security Policy (CFSP)

Following on from earlier efforts, since the early 1970s, at co-operation in the area of foreign policy, the Common Foreign and Security Policy was established as the "second pillar" of the European Union in the 1992 Treaty on European Union, signed at Maastricht. The common policy exists in parallel to the separate foreign and security policies of the EU Member States. A number of important changes were introduced in the Amsterdam Treaty, which came into force in 1999, and since then there have been numerous developments in Common Foreign and Security Policy, including under the Nice Treaty.

The common policy is concerned with foreign affairs of a political character where the Member States judge that the broad objectives they share can more effectively be achieved by acting together or by co-ordinating their actions rather than by acting separately or in an unco-ordinated fashion. The draft Constitutional Treaty contains extensive provisions on Common Foreign and Security Policy, some pre-existing, some new, which are summarised in the Forum's summary.

Community Method (Community Way)

The "Community method" is the method which describes the institutional set-up brought into being by the Treaty of Rome which invented a unique way of defining relations between sovereign states of unequal size who agree to pool sovereignty. In practice, the Community method involves pooling sovereignty; an ongoing dialogue to identify the common interest; majority decisions usually; negotiations taking place within a strict institutional structure where the European Commission alone has the right to propose European legislation and where decisions are taken in a number of different ways but all involving an interaction between the Council of Ministers and the European Parliament; and decisions being open to challenge before a supranational court whose judgments override national law in the domains covered by the EU.

Confer Competences / Principle of Conferral

The principle of conferral means that the Union does not have general competences in its own right, but only those that are specifically conferred upon it by the Member States in the founding treaties and their subsequent modifications. The Union can only act on the basis of a provision of the treaties that authorises it to do so. In treaty terms, competence means the legal capacity or ability to legislate or to take other action.

Conferred Powers

This refers to the principle whereby the EU has only the powers conferred on its institutions by the treaties. Powers not conferred remain with the Member States.

Constitution

The body of fundamental principles or established precedents according to which a state or other organisation is governed—usually, but not always, set out in writing in a series of articles contained in a basic document.

Convergence

Becoming more alike or closer together in terms of various characteristics or capabilities.

Council of Europe
The Council of Europe is an intergovernmental organisation, set up in 1948, which includes in its aims the protection of human rights and the promotion and awareness of Europe's cultural identity and diversity. It has a wider membership than the EU. Though all Member States of the EU are also members of the Council of Europe, the latter is a distinct organisation in its own right.

Council of Ministers
The Council of Ministers is the EU institution in which the governments of the Member States are represented. The Council consists of one representative of each Member State at Ministerial level. The Council meets in a whole range of formations, mainly sectoral (e.g. the Ministers for Agriculture when the Council takes decisions on the Common Agricultural Policy). The President (or chair) of the Council is the Minister of the Member State currently holding the Presidency of the EU. Up to now, this was for a six-month term according to an agreed and equal rotation. The draft Constitutional Treaty proposes some changes in regard to the Council of Ministers, which are summarised in the Forum's summary.

Degressively Proportional
This refers to a system of representation of EU Member States in the European Parliament, whereby the number of seats a country has is broadly proportional to the size of its population but with the ratio between the number of seats and the population size being progressively more favourable the smaller the size of a country's population.

Delegated Regulation
Under the proposals in the draft Constitutional Treaty, where there are non-essential elements to a European law or a European framework law, these laws may delegate to the European Commission the power to enact detailed regulations to supplement or amend these elements. The objective, content, scope and duration of these delegations has to be defined in

the original law or framework law. The Council of Ministers and the European Parliament are to supervise the use of this power and may also revoke any such delegation.

Direct Universal Suffrage
Election directly under a system where all persons of voting age are eligible to vote.

Economic, Social and Territorial Cohesion
This means balanced and sustainable development, reducing economic, social and infrastructural inequalities between regions and countries and promoting equal opportunities for all individuals. In practical terms, the EU seeks to achieve these aims by means of a variety of financing operations, principally through the Structural Funds.

Enhanced Co-operation
Enhanced co-operation is the term used to describe a specific EU provision, first introduced in the Treaty of Amsterdam (1997), which allows groups of Member States fewer than the entire membership of the Union to avail of the institutions of the Union in order to undertake closer co-operation between themselves. The Nice Treaty sets out in a consolidated format the pre-conditions for autho-risation of enhanced co-operation. The draft Constitutional Treaty proposes some changes in regard to what has applied up to now, as regards Enhanced Co-operation. These are summarised in the Forum's summary.

European Armaments Agency
Under the draft Constitutional Treaty proposed by the Convention, a European Armaments, Research and Military Capabilities Agency would be established and Member States would have the option of participating in it or not, as they choose. Among its proposed functions would be to monitor the capability commitments of Member States, promote harmonisation of pro-curement and support defence technology research.

European Commission

The European Commission is one of the EU institutions. It was created as an independent body to represent the European interest common to all Member States. As things stand now, the 20 members of the Commission are drawn from the 15 EU countries, but they each swear an oath of independence, distancing themselves from partisan influence from any source. The Commission is the driving force in the legislative process, proposing the legislation on which the European Parliament and the Council of Ministers make decisions. The draft Constitutional Treaty proposes changes in regard to the Commission. These are summarised in the Forum's summary.   *http://europa.eu.int/comm/index_en.htm*

European Council

The European Council is the term used to describe the institution within which the Heads of State or Government of the European Union Member States meet regularly. It meets at least twice a year—more recently, about four times- and the President of the European Commission attends as a full member. Its functions are to give the EU the impetus it needs in order to develop and to define general policy guidelines and priorities. The draft Constitutional Treaty proposes changes in regard to the European Council. These are summarised in the Forum's summary.

European Convention on Human Rights (ECHR)

The European Convention on Human Rights and Fundamental Freedoms, signed in 1950 under the aegis of the Council of Europe, sets out a list of human rights, which the participating countries guarantee to respect and uphold. The Convention established, for the first time, a system of international protection for human rights offering individuals the possibility of applying to a dedicated international court—the European Court of Human Rights—for the enforcement of their rights. All Members States of the Union have ratified the Convention. The draft Constitutional Treaty envisages that the Union, as such, would seek to join the Convention.

European Court of Auditors

The Court of Auditors is an institution that acts like the auditors of a business or other organisation. It monitors the Union's accounts, examining the legality and regularity of the revenue and expenditure in the budget and ensuring sound financial management.   *http://www.eca.eu.int/*

European Court of Justice

This is the institution responsible for interpreting and enforcing Community law. The Court has one judge from each Member State. It has jurisdiction in disputes between Member States, between the Union and its Member States and between institutions and private individuals and the Union about matters that fall within the remit of the EU or are regulated by EU legislation or decisions.   *http://curia.eu.int/en/index.htm*

Eurojust

The European Judicial Co-operation Unit. A body of national prosecutors, magistrates or police officers from the Member States, established in 2002 under the Treaty of Nice to co-ordinate the fight against crime. The draft Constitutional Treaty proposes some changes in respect of Eurojust and its work. These are referred to in the Forum's summary.

Europol

European Police Office, established under an agreement reached in 1995 and which entered into force on 1 October 1998, but only became fully operational on 1 July 1999. Europol's headquarters are in The Hague and it co-ordinates police co-operation throughout the EU in particular, agreed areas, for example in the areas of drug trafficking, clandestine immigration networks, trafficking in stolen vehicles, trafficking in human beings (including child pornography), counterfeiting currency and falsification of other means of payment, trafficking in radioactive and nuclear substances, terrorism and money-laundering. The draft Constitutional Treaty proposes some changes in respect of Europol and its work. These are referred to in the Forum's summary.

European Decision
A European Decision is the name proposed in the draft Constitutional Treaty for an EU non-legislative act, which is binding in its entirety. A decision which specifies those to whom it is addressed is binding only on them.

European Law
A European Law, under the simplification proposals of the draft Constitutional Treaty, would be the new term for what, up to now, was called a Regulation. It refers to a legislative act, which has general application, is binding in its entirety and applies directly in all Member States, i.e. without the need for any further steps by the Member States.

European Framework Law
A European Framework Law, under the simplification proposals of the draft Constitutional Treaty, would be the new term for what used to be called a Directive and would be a legislative act which is binding as to the result to be achieved on the Member States to which it is addressed, but leaves national authorities free to decide the forms and means to achieve that result.

European Ombudsman
The office of the European Ombudsman is empowered to receive and investigate complaints from any citizen of the Union or any natural or legal person residing in a Member State concerning instances of alleged bad or unfair administration in the activities of the Community institutions or bodies and to follow up and report on the outcomes.

European Opinion
A European Opinion is, under the Convention's simplification proposals, the name for a form of non-binding legal act of the Union.

European Parliament
The European Parliament is the EU institution that represents the citizens of the Member States. It currently consists of 626 members directly

elected by the electorates in constituencies in the 15 Member States. In many areas, the Parliament acts as co-legislator with the European Council. The Parliament and the Council of Ministers jointly constitute the budgetary authority. The draft Constitutional Treaty contains a number of proposals affecting the make-up and powers of the parliament. These changes are summarised in the Forum's summary. *http://www.europarl.eu.int*

European Recommendation
A European Recommendation is under the Convention's simplification proposals, the name for a form of non-binding legal act of the Union.

European Regulation
A European Regulation is, under the Convention's simplification proposals, the name for a form of non-legislative act relating to implementation, which can be binding in its entirety or binding as regards the results to be achieved.

European Security and Defence Policy (ESDP)
Established in 1999 at the Cologne European Council, the ESDP aims to allow the Union to develop its civilian and military capacities for crisis management and conflict prevention at international level, thus helping to maintain peace and international security, in accordance with the United Nations Charter.

Flexibility Clause
The flexibility clause within the draft Constitutional Treaty, the antecedents of which go back to the Treaty of Rome, allows flexible adjustments of EU competence within the defined remit of the Union. The existing clause can only be used in connection with the common market. The new clause will allow flexibility in all areas of the EU.

Freedom of Establishment
Every EU citizen, through freedom of establishment, is allowed to set up a business in any EU country in the same way and on the same legal basis as a national of that country.

Geneva Convention of 28 July 1951
UN rules on asylum dating from 1951. They give every refugee the right to have an application for asylum at least considered by the country in which they apply.

Harmonisation
This means co-ordinating national policies, rules and technical standards so closely that products and services, capital and labour can move freely throughout the EU.

In Camera
This is a term, taken from Latin, meaning "in private".

Intergovernmental Conference (IGC)
This is the term used to describe the only arena in which, through negotiations between the EU Member States' governments, amendments to the treaties can be agreed. The next IGC will commence on 4 October 2003.

Judicially Cognisable
This refers to the kind of things that judges or courts may, under the law or established legal procedure, take account of in the course of legal proceedings.

Languages of the Constitution
This refers to the languages in which the Constitution proposed by the Convention is to be drawn up, each version being equally authentic, as set out in Article IV-10, the last article of the draft Constitutional Treaty: the list includes the Irish language.

Legal Base
In order for the EU to have power to act in any area, that area must have what is known as a "legal base" in the treaty structure. Any areas where the EU is to have such power must be recognised formally and explicitly

in the legal structure of the treaties. The draft Constitutional Treaty maintains all areas where there were legal bases previously and creates legal bases in some further, limited areas.

Legal Continuity

This refers to the need to ensure that when a legal entity ceases to exist or to operate, the rights and obligations, assets and liabilities, which had been attached to it or assumed by it and which continue to be relevant, do not cease to have legal force as a result of the entity's demise but instead are taken over and continued in being under a new legal entity which succeeds to the role and functions of the defunct body. In the context of the draft Constitutional Treaty, this relates to the proposed repeal of the previous treaties and their replacement by the proposed Constitutional Treaty and the consequent absorption of previous entities by the European Union and the need to ensure that the latter continues to be vested with rights and obligations, assets and liabilities arising from the previous treaties.

Legal Personality

The question of the Union's legal status has arisen primarily in connection with its lack of capacity to conclude treaties or accede to agreements or conventions that have binding legal force. Legally, Member States are joined in two separate communities each with individual legal status (European Community and Euratom). Up to now, only these entities or Member States of them, individually, could conclude or accede to international agreements. Under the new draft Constitutional Treaty the European Union would replace the previous entities and accordingly the draft Treaty proposes that the EU, as such, would henceforth carry legal personality and thus have the treaty-making powers mentioned above.

Legislative Act

An act making primary law for or within the EU: this includes European laws and European framework laws.

Legitimacy

This is a political concept, relating to whether, or how far, a political system or a set of political arrangements or institutions is regarded as being valid and worthy of acceptance or support by the people who are governed under such arrangements or whose lives are affected by what is done by the institutions.

Lisbon Process or Strategy

Launched at an EU summit in Lisbon, Portugal in 2000, the Lisbon Process or Strategy is a voluntary co-ordination (often referred to as the Open Method of Co-ordination) of a whole range of economic, social and sectoral policies among Member States. It aims to make the EU the most competitive and knowledge-based economy in the world by 2010.

Mutual Recognition

Instead of harmonisation i.e. making standards within the EU fully consistent by imposing a common, cross-EU law, the EU often uses the method of "mutual recognition" of standards. This means that a national standard in one country—for example regarding what specifications a product must have—is accepted as being valid in all.

National Mandate

This refers to a job or position in an institution of government at national level, such as a parliament, government or court.

Official Journal of the European Union

This refers to a daily publication setting out the official acts of the EU, such as the laws it has passed, decisions it has taken, contracts it is offering for tender, jobs for which it wants to recruit etc.

Ordinary Legislative Procedure

The form of decision making process where the Council of Ministers and the European Parliament carry out legislative functions on an equal footing (co-decision), on the basis of proposals that, legally, can only be made by the European Commission, is described in the new draft Constitutional Treaty as "Ordinary Legislative Procedure".

Petersberg Tasks

In the Maastricht Treaty of 1992, the Member States of the European Union undertook to enhance co-operation on international affairs through the Common Foreign and Security Policy. The Treaty of Amsterdam, 1997 reflects new priorities of humanitarian, rescue, peacekeeping and crisis management tasks — the Petersberg tasks (called after a place in Germany where agreement on them was reached)— by incorporating these tasks into the European Union's Common Foreign and Security Policy. The draft Constitutional Treaty extends the tasks to cover joint disarmament operations, military advice and post-conflict stabilisation.

Phytosanitary

This is a term for the field of plant health.

Praesidium

This is the term, taken from Latin, for the committee or group which steered the business of the Convention.

Precautionary Principle

This refers to a principle, adopted by the UN Conference on the Environment and Development (1992), that in order to protect the environment, a precautionary approach should be widely applied, meaning that where there are threats of serious or irreversible damage to the environment, lack of full scientific certainty should not be used as a reason for postponing cost-effective measures to prevent environmental degradation.

Principle of Loyal Co-operation

The principle which commits the Union and its individual Member States to assist each other in carrying out tasks, common or co-ordinated, which flow from the obligations they have assumed and refrain from acting in ways that would block or impede discharge of those tasks.

Principle of Non-Refoulement

The legal principle of non-refoulement is binding on all states as a matter of customary international law and is expressly included in the Irish Refugee Act. Non-refoulement prohibits states from sending a person back to a country in which they may face serious human rights abuses.

Protocol

A protocol is a legal text, which is usually added (annexed) to a treaty and which deals in a more detailed way with a certain topic e.g. in the draft Constitutional Treaty there is a protocol on subsidiarity and the role of national parliaments. A protocol to a treaty has the same legal status as the treaty itself when it has been ratified by the Member States.

Qualified Majority Voting (QMV)

QMV is the form of decision-making used for most Council of Ministers decisions. A decision requires a specified minimum number of votes in favour that is more than one half plus one. Each Member State is assigned a number of votes. These are allocated on a basis broadly proportional to population size but on a cluster basis, under which Member States with broadly similar populations are given the same number of votes. For example, Ireland currently has 3 votes, the same as Finland and Denmark. In the present EU of 15 Member States, a qualified majority is 62 out of 87 votes. The draft Constitutional Treaty proposes changes in regard to both the requirements for, and the scope of application of, QMV. These are summarised in the Forum's summary.

Ratification

In the context of the Treaties, this is the process by which each individual Member State formally decides, through their own national procedures, in each case, that the Treaty, previously signed on their behalf, will be legally binding on them, thereby allowing the European Union to put into force the articles of the Treaty. All Member States must ratify EU treaties in order for them to come into force.

Reasoned Opinion

The European Commission scrutinises steps taken by each Member State to implement EU law and, if dissatisfied, may issue what is known as a "reasoned opinion" to Member States governments. This is a sort of "early warning system" within which the Commission outlines the measures that will need to be taken in order for the Member State(s) to fully implement the EU law in question. Should these measures not be taken, then the Commission refers the matter to the European Court of Justice.

A second meaning of the term arises in the protocol on applying the principles of proportionality (see page 15). There, the term refers to an opinion with reasons, put forward by a national parliament or a chamber therof, that a proposal for a law, made by the Commission, is in breach of the principle of subsidiarity. In this case, a reasoned opinion is part of an "early warning system", to be operated by national parliaments.

Right of Initiative

Reflecting its role as guardian of the treaties and defender of the general interest, the European Commission has been given the "right of initiative" which empowers and requires it to make proposals on the matters contained in the Treaty, either because the Treaty expressly so provides or because the Commission considers it necessary.

Currently, the right of initiative is exclusive to the Commission in all areas of Union activity except Common Foreign and Security Policy, where Member States *also* have the right to make proposals and some areas of Justice and Home Affairs where *only* Member States may make proposals. The draft Constitutional Treaty proposes changes in regard to who has the right of initiative in different areas. These are summarised in the Forum's summary.

Services of General Interest
This is an expression in the treaties to describe telecommunications, water, postal, transport services and other infrastructure in the Member States, as well as education, health, that are widely regarded as basic necessities for a satisfactory life under modern conditions in Europe.

Social Market Economy
This refers to the type of economic model that has characterised the countries in the European Union since reconstruction after the Second World War, in which the economy is primarily based on the competitive operation of the market but with significant regulation in the public interest and in addition, in most cases, a significant consultative role for the social partners in the management of the economy and, in some countries, also at firm level.

Special Legislative Procedure
A number of areas outlined in the Treaty lie outside the remit of the Ordinary Legislative Procedure described above and fall under what is described in the draft Constitutional Treaty as "Special Legislative Procedure". Decision-making procedures vary and may allow for a dominant role for either the Council of Ministers or the European Parliament. In some cases, proposals may come from sources other than the Commission. Unanimity is also allowed for in some cases.

Stability and Growth Pact
An agreement introduced in the lead-up to monetary union, the aim of the Stability and Growth Pact is to ensure that the Member States continued their budgetary discipline efforts once the single currency was introduced. The pact details technical arrangements on surveillance of budgetary positions as well as co-ordination of economic policies and implementation of an excessive deficit procedure, allowing the Council to penalise any participating Member State which fails to take appropriate measures to end an excessive budget deficit. In the medium, term the

Member States have undertaken to pursue the objective of a balanced or nearly balanced budget.

Subsidiary Protection

The term used for the protection given to certain categories of persecuted people, who are not covered by the 1951 Geneva Convention on refugees but nevertheless in need of international protection.

Supranational

Transcending national limits or boundaries. In the context of the EU, the term usually refers to the institutions that exist to pursue the common European Union interests, shared by the Member States. It also refers to the discharge of functions and exercise of powers by those institutions, transcending national boundaries, in the domains where the Member States, in the treaties, have conferred those functions and powers on them. The supranational approach is often contrasted with the intergovernmental approach that involves keeping supranational institutions, and their role, to a minimum.

Sustainable Development

A form of economic growth, which is based on, the most economical use of resources, particularly those that are scarce and which is thus more likely to satisfy society's needs over the long term, rather than using the resources rapidly in the short term. The concept is founded on the assumption that development, while meeting today's needs or tomorrow's, must do so without jeopardising the prospects of future generations.

Transparency

Making it possible to see clearly and to follow from outside the way in which decisions are reached.

EUROPEAN UNION TREATY AND ENLARGEMENT HISTORY

1951
European Coal and Steel
Community (ECSC)
Treaty of Paris

1957
European Economic Community
(EEC)
European Atomic Energy Community
The Treaties of Rome
Founder Members
Belgium, France, Germany, Italy,
Luxembourg, The Netherlands

1973
Denmark, Ireland, United
Kingdom

1981
Greece

1986
Single European Act
Portugal, Spain

1992
Treaty on European Union
Maastricht Treaty

1995
Austria, Finland, Sweden

1997
Amsterdam Treaty

2002
Nice Treaty

2004
Cyprus, Czech Republic, Estonia,
Hungary, Latvia, Lithuania, Malta,
Poland, Slovenia, Slovakia